Praise

numbers 1 - 150

FALCON BOOKS LONDON

YOUTH PRAISE

1

We will sing of our Redeemer, He's our King:
All His glory, all His praise to you we bring;
With our hearts and with our voices Him we sing,
We love the Lord, we love His Word, He's our
King.

2

Start with chorus
Come and praise the Lord our King, Hallelujah.
Come and praise the Lord our King, Hallelujah.

1 Christ was born in Bethlehem, Hallelujah,
Son of God and Son of Man, Hallelujah:
Chorus

2 He grew up an earthly child, Hallelujah,
Of the world, but undefiled, Hallelujah:
Chorus

3 Jesus died at Calvary, Hallelujah,
Rose again triumphantly, Hallelujah:
Chorus

4 He will cleanse us from our sin, Hallelujah,
If we live by faith in Him, Hallelujah:
Chorus

5 We will live with Him one day, Hallelujah,
And for ever with Him stay, Hallelujah:
Chorus

3

1 Tell out, my soul, the greatness of the Lord;
Unnumbered blessings give my spirit voice;
Tender to me the promise of His Word;
In God my Saviour shall my heart rejoice.

2 Tell out, my soul, the greatness of His Name!
Make known His might, the deeds His arm has done;
His mercy sure, from age to age the same;
His Holy Name—the Lord, the Mighty One.

3 Tell out, my soul, the greatness of His might!
Powers and dominions lay their glory by.
Proud hearts and stubborn wills are put to flight,
The hungry fed, the humble lifted high.

4 Tell out, my soul, the glories of His Word!
Firm is His promise, and His mercy sure.
Tell out, my soul, the greatness of the Lord
To children's children and for evermore!

4

There's no greater Name than Jesus,
Name of Him who came to save us,
In that saving Name of Jesus
Every knee should bow.

Let ev'rything that is 'neath the ground,
Let ev'rything in the world around,
Let ev'rything that's high o'er the sky
Bow at Jesus' Name.

In our minds by faith professing,
In our hearts by inward blessing,
On our tongues by words confessing,
Jesus Christ is Lord!

Ewart Keep with every hope for the future, from the world's most successful failure!

5

1 When morning gilds the skies,
My heart awaking cries,
'May Jesus Christ be praised!'
Alike at work and prayer
To Jesus I repair:
'May Jesus Christ be praised!'

2 Be this, when day is past,
Of all my thoughts the last,
'May Jesus Christ be praised!'
The night becomes as day,
When from the heart we say:
'May Jesus Christ be praised!'

3 Does sadness fill my mind?
A solace here I find,
'May Jesus Christ be praised!'
When evil thoughts molest,
With this I shield my breast:
'May Jesus Christ be praised!'

4 To God, the Word on high,
The hosts of angels cry,
'May Jesus Christ be praised!'
Let mortals, too, upraise
Their voice in hymns of praise:
'May Jesus Christ be praised!'

5 Let earth's wide circle round
In joyful notes resound,
'May Jesus Christ be praised!'
Let earth and sea and sky,
From depth to height, reply:
'May Jesus Christ be praised!'

6 Be this while life is mine,
My canticle divine,
'May Jesus Christ be praised!'
Be this the eternal song,
Through all the ages long:
'May Jesus Christ be praised!'

6

There is joy in the presence of the angels of God
Over one sinner that repenteth.
There is joy in the presence of the angels of God
Over one sinner that repenteth.
For the Son of Man is come to seek,
To seek and to save that which was lost.
There is joy in the presence of the angels of God
Over one sinner that repenteth,
Praise the Lord for His love and for His heaven above,
Where His saints shall rejoice for ever.

7

1 I'm singing for my Lord everywhere I go,
Singing of His wondrous love that the world may know
How He saved a wretch like me by His death on Calvary,
I'm singing for my Lord everywhere I go.

2 I'm singing, but sometimes heavy is the rod,
For this world is not a friend to the grace of God;
Yet I sing the whole day long, for He fills my heart with song,
I'm singing for my Lord everywhere I go.

3 I'm singing for the lost just because I know
Jesus Christ, whose precious blood washes white as snow;
If my songs to Him can bring some lost soul I'll gladly sing:
I'm singing for my Lord everywhere I go.

4 I'm singing, for the saints as they journey home;
Soon they'll reach that happy land where they'll never roam,
And with me they'll join and sing praises to our Lord and King:
I'm singing for my Lord everywhere I go.

8

Sweet is the work, my God, my King,
To praise Thy Name, give thanks and sing,
To show Thy love by morning light,
And talk of all Thy truth at night.

9

1 We sing a loving Jesus
Who left His throne above
And came to earth to ransom
The children of His love;
It is an oft-told story,
And yet we love to tell
How Christ, the King of glory
Once deigned with man to dwell.

2 We sing a lowly Jesus
No kingly crown He had
His heart was bowed with anguish
His face was marred and sad;
In deep humiliation
He came, His work to do;
O Lord of our salvation
Let us be humble too.

3 We sing a mighty Jesus
Whose voice could raise the dead
The sightless eyes He opened
The famished souls He fed.
Thou camest to deliver
Mankind from sin and shame;
Redeemer and life-giver,
We praise Thy Holy Name!

4 We sing a coming Jesus
The time is drawing near
When Christ with all His angels
In glory shall appear.
Lord, save us, we entreat Thee,
In this Thy day of grace,
That we may gladly meet Thee,
And see Thee face to face.

10

1 Christ triumphant ever reigning,
Saviour, Master, King,
Lord of heav'n, our lives sustaining,
Hear us as we sing.
Yours the glory and the crown—
The high renown—
The eternal name.

2 Word incarnate, truth revealing,
Son of Man on earth,
Power and majesty concealing
By Your humble birth.
Yours the glory and the crown—
The high renown—
The eternal name.

3 Suffering servant, scorned, ill-treated,
Victim crucified,
Death is through the cross defeated
Sinners justified.
Yours the glory and the crown—
The high renown—
The eternal name.

4 Priestly King, enthroned for ever
High in heaven above,
Sin and death and hell shall never
Stifle hymns of love.
Yours the glory and the crown—
The high renown—
The eternal name.

5 So, our hearts and voices raising
Through the ages long,
Ceaselessly upon You gazing
This shall be our song.
Yours the glory and the crown—
The high renown—
The eternal name.

Åse Beate Eskeland
Norway (Vange)
Rom 8,37-39.

Ps. 23
Your sister in Jesus Inge Gabel

11

1 Lord of the cross of shame,
Set my cold heart aflame
With love for You, my Saviour and my Master;
Who on that lonely day
Bore all my sins away,
And saved me from the judgement and disaster.

2 Lord of the empty tomb,
Born of a virgin's womb,
Triumphant over death, its power defeated;
How gladly now I sing
Your praise, my risen King,
And worship You, in heaven's splendour seated.

3 Lord of my life today,
Teach me to live and pray
As one who knows the joy of sins forgiven;
So may I ever be,
Now and eternally,
United with the citizens of heaven.

12

1 He who now is reigning in majesty
Stooped to bear our sin in humility,
There on Calvary—Jesus died for me—
Died to set me free—eternally!

Chorus
Jesus Christ is my Lord and King,
To Him honour and glory bring,
Join the mighty host in heav'n above
and praise His gracious Name.

2 Justified by faith we have peace with God,
Fellowship with Him through our Saviour's blood,
Wonder though it be—sons of God are we—
In His family—eternally!
Chorus

13

Thank You for ev'ry new good morning,
Thank You for ev'ry fresh new day,
Thank You that I may cast my burdens
Wholly onto You.

Thank You for ev'ry friend I have, Lord,
Thank You for ev'ryone I know,
Thank You when I can feel forgiveness
To my greatest foe.

Thank You for leisure and employment,
Thank You for ev'ry heartfelt joy,
Thank You for all that makes me happy
And for melody.

Thank You for ev'ry shade and sorrow,
Thank You for comfort in Your Word,
Thank You that I am guided by You
Ev'rywhere I go.

Thank You for grace to know Your gospel,
Thank You for all Your Spirit's power,
Thank You for Your unfailing love which
Reaches far and near.

Thank You for free and full salvation,
Thank You for grace to hold it fast,
Thank You, O Lord, I want to thank You,
That I'm free to thank!

14

Oh, thank the Lord, oh thank the Lord,
Give Him the praise for He is good;
Because His mercy does endure,
His faithfulness is ever sure;
Oh thank the Lord, oh thank the Lord,
Give Him the praise for He is good.

Mark 14,35. Ann Lancaster

15

1 O Lord most high, Thou holy God and Saviour,
Thy pow'r and might are more than tongue can tell,
But greater far the love that planned salvation
And saved the lost from sin and death and hell.

Chorus
O God of Love, O God of Calvary,
How great Thou art! How great Thou art!
In all the world there is no one like Thee,
How great Thou art! How great Thou art!

2 Once far from God, an alien and a stranger,
Of hope bereft, a sinner lost and lone,
But Jesus came to rescue from the danger,
To give us life He sacrificed His own.
Chorus

3 In mercy rich, in love and grace abounding,
When we were dead in trespasses and sins,
Thine only Son for us was freely given,
How great Thou art! in Thee our life begins.
Chorus

16

Open Thou my eyes, O Lord,
Open Thou my eyes, O Lord;
That I may see the wondrous things of Thy law,
Wondrous things of Thy law,
Wondrous things of Thy law,
Open Thou my eyes.

17

Lord, You look with goodness on us,
Lord, You pour Your love upon us,
And You promise in Your Word
To hear us when we pray.

18

Come among us, Lord,
Gathered round Thy Word,
To mind and heart Thy truth impart
O living Word.
In this morning (evening) hour,
Lord, reveal Thy power!
May souls be fed with living bread:
Come among us, Lord!

19

By blue Galilee Jesus walked of old,
By blue Galilee wondrous things He told.
Saviour, still my teacher be,
Showing wondrous things to me,
As of old by Galilee, blue Galilee.

20

Turn you eyes upon Jesus,
Look full in His wonderful face;
And the things of earth will grow strangely dim
In the light of His glory and grace.

May God bless you and we'll meet again in Heaven if not before!
Cathy
Königswinter '74.

21

Break Thou the Bread of Life, dear Lord, to me,
As Thou didst break the loaves beside the sea;
Beyond the sacred page I seek Thee, Lord;
My spirit longs for Thee, O living Word!

22

Speak to us, Lord, in this brief hour today;
Give light upon the written word we pray;
Stir heart and mind to heed and to obey,
For this we plead.

23

Triumphant victor, life-giving Saviour,
Ris'n from the dead on that first Easter day.
Make known Thy power, Lord, to each one here, Lord,
Thou risen Son of God, we own Thy sway.

24

God's love is wonderful, God's love is wonderful,
Wonderful that He should give His Son to die for me,
God's love is wonderful.

25

On Calv'ry's tree He died for me,
That I His love might know.
To set me free He died for me,
That's why I love Him so.

26

1 Wonderful grace of Jesus, greater than all my sin;
How shall my tongue describe it, where shall its praise begin?
Taking away my burden, setting my spirit free,
For the wonderful grace of Jesus reaches me.

Chorus
Wonderful the matchless grace of Jesus,
Deeper than the mighty rolling sea:
Higher than the mountain, sparkling like a fountain,
All sufficient grace for even me.
Broader than the scope of my transgressions,
Greater far than all my sin and shame,
Oh, magnify the precious Name of Jesus,
Praise His Name!

2 Wonderful grace of Jesus, reaching to all the lost;
By it I have been pardoned, saved to the uttermost
Chains have been torn asunder, giving me liberty.
For the wonderful grace of Jesus reaches me:
Chorus

3 Wonderful grace of Jesus, reaching the most defiled
By its transforming power, making him God's own child,
Purchasing peace and heaven, for all eternity,
And the wonderful grace of Jesus reaches me:
Chorus

27

Higher than the hills, deeper than the sea,
Broader than the skies above is my Redeemer's love for me;
To His cross of shame, Jesus freely came,
Bearing all my sin and sorrow—Wondrous love!

28

1 In the garden Gethsemane
Christ Jesus knelt alone;
With burdened heart and pain ahead
He faced the cross alone;
Never was a man forsaken
In such a way as this:
In the garden Gethsemane
Christ Jesus knelt alone.

2 In the garden Gethsemane
Christ Jesus knelt alone,
Yet where were His disciples when
He faced the cross alone?
Eyes were heavy, sleep was easy,
They let Him watch alone:
In the garden Gethsemane
Christ Jesus knelt alone.

3 In the garden Gethsemane
Christ Jesus knelt alone,
'Father', He said, 'Thy will be done'
Christ Jesus knelt alone;
Then the cross for our salvation
For us then to atone:
In the garden Gethsemane
Christ Jesus knelt alone.

4 In the garden Gethsemane
Christ Jesus knelt alone,
And now today He looks to us,
To those He calls His own;
Are we watching? Are we praying?
Or are we failing Him?
In the garden Gethsemane
Christ Jesus knelt alone.

29

The grace of the Lord, like a fathomless sea,
Sufficient for you, sufficient for me,
Is tender and patient and boundless and free,
Sufficient for ev'ry need.

30

Living, He loved me;
Dying, He saved me;
Buried, He carried my sins far away;
Rising, He justified
Freely for ever;
One day He's coming,
O glorious day!

31

For God so loved the world, He gave His only Son,
To die on Calvary's tree, from sin to set me free;
Some day He's coming back, what glory that will be,
Wonderful His love to me.

32

1 It was just two thousand years ago
He walked thro' Galilee,
The eternal God had stepped below
In human form to be;
Born of a lowly Hebrew maid,
A carpenter He was by trade;
He came down,
Two thousand years ago:

Chorus

They tell of Jesus' glory,
Who met Him in the way;
And it is no idle story,
For He lives in me today;
He gives me peace and purpose true,
A power that's old, but ever new;
God came down,
Two thousand years ago.

2 It was just two thousand years ago
He died on Calvary;
It was for sin He suffered so,
Though innocent was He.
My sin and guilt lay on His head;
My penalty He bore instead;
He suffered,
Two thousand years ago:

Chorus

3 It was just two thousand years ago
An empty tomb was found;
The stone was rolled away we know,
The powers of hell are bound;
My risen Lord is now on high,
He lives that we may never die,
He triumphed!
Two thousand years ago:

Chorus

33

Oh, the love that drew salvation's plan!
Oh, the grace that brought it down to man!
Oh, the mighty gulf that God did span at Calvary!
Mercy there was great, and grace was free;
Pardon there was multiplied to me;
There my burdened soul found liberty, at Calvary.

34

1 Just because He set His heart on me,
Just because His pow'r could set me free,
Just because of my iniquity,
Jesus died.

2 When by Him the ransom was supplied,
When by Him the debt was satisfied,
When by Him we could be justified,
Jesus rose.

3 Now of Calvary each Christian sings,
Now with praise to Christ all heaven rings,
Now He's Lord of Lords and King of Kings.
Jesus reigns.

35

His compassions fail not, fail not,
His compassions fail not, they are new ev'ry morning,
Great is Thy faithfulness, great is Thy faithfulness;
His compassions fail not, they are new ev'ry day.

36

Christine M. Embry.

1 Can it be true, the things they say of You?
You walked this earth sharing with friends You knew,
All that they had the work, the joy, the pain,
That we might find the way to heav'n again.

2 And day by day You still return this way;
But we recall there was a debt to pay:
Out of Your love for Your own world above,
You left that holy thing, Your endless love to prove.

3 Can it be true, the things they did to You –
The death, the shame, and were Your friends so few?
Yet You returned again alive and free –
Can it be true, my Lord, it had to be?

37

I know a fount where sins are wash'd away;
I know a place where night is turned to day;
Burdens are lifted, blind eyes made to see:
There's a wonder working pow'r in the blood of Calvary.

38

1 Tell me, Lord Jesus;
Why did You have to die, Master?
Tell me Lord Jesus:
Why did You have to die?

Chorus
And You came down to earth,
From heaven willingly,
There at Calvary.
On the cursed tree,
There You died for me,
There You died for me.

2 Pride, sin and wrong in us,
That cut us off from God, our Father,
When we were bound in sin,
That's when You came to die.
Chorus

3 You came to set us free,
That's why You had to die, Master,
To give us liberty,
That's why You had to die.
Chorus

39

1 New! ev'ry morning it's new!
The love of God to me is wonderfully new!
New! ev'ry morning it's new!
The mercy of the Lord is wonderfully new!
Great is His faithfulness, constant is His love,
Great is His saving pow'r coming from above.

2 New! ev'ry morning it's new!
The love of Calvary is wonderfully new!
New! ev'ry morning it's new!
The mercy fresh outpoured is wonderfully new!
He is our daily strength, He's our daily guide
If we will wait on Him and in Him abide!

3 New! ev'ry morning it's new!
The love of God to me is wonderfully new!
New! ev'ry morning it's new!
The mercy of the Lord is wonderfully new!

40

1 Jesu, lover of my soul,
Let me to Thy bosom fly,
While the nearer waters roll,
While the tempest still is high,
Hide me, O my Saviour, hide,
Till the storm of life is past;
Safe into the haven guide;
O receive my soul at last!

2 Other refuge have I none;
Hangs my helpless soul on Thee;
Leave, ah, leave me not alone;
Still support and comfort me.
All my trust on Thee is stayed;
All my help from Thee I bring;
Cover my defenceless head
With the shadow of Thy wing.

3 Thou, O Christ, art all I want;
More than all in Thee I find;
Raise the fallen, cheer the faint,
Heal the sick and lead the blind.
Just and holy is Thy name,
I am all unrighteousness;
False and full of sin I am,
Thou art full of truth and grace.

4 Plenteous grace with Thee is found.
Grace to cover all my sin;
Let the healing streams abound;
Make and keep me pure within.
Thou of life the fountain art,
Freely let me take of Thee;
Spring Thou up within my heart,
Rise to all eternity.

41

1 Ride on, ride on in majesty!
Hark, all the tribes Hosanna cry;
O Saviour meek, pursue Thy road
With palms and scattered garments strowed.

2 Ride on, ride on in majesty!
In lowly pomp ride on to die;
O Christ, Thy triumphs now begin
O'er captive death and conquered sin.

3 Ride on, ride on in majesty!
The angel armies of the sky
Look down with sad and wondering eyes
To see the approaching sacrifice.

4 Ride on, ride on in majesty!
Thy last, Thy fiercest strife is nigh;
The Father on His sapphire throne
Awaits His own anointed Son.

5 Ride on, ride on in majesty!
In lowly pomp ride on to die;
Bow Thy meek head to mortal pain,
Then take, O God, Thy power, and reign.

42

Jesus died for me, His blood has made me free.
Now He lives within me and He leads the way;
While I trust in Him I've vict'ry over sin:
Praise His Name He loves me so, and He shall be my King.

43

1 There is a Name I love to hear,
I love to speak its worth;
It sounds like music in my ear,
The sweetest Name on earth:

Chorus
Oh, how I love the Saviour's Name,
Oh, how I love the Saviour's Name,
Oh, how I love the Saviour's Name,
The sweetest Name on earth.

2 It tells me of a Saviour's love,
Who died to set me free;
It tells me of His precious blood,
The sinner's perfect plea:
Chorus

3 It tells of one wnose loving heart
Can feel my deepest woe,
Who in my sorrow bears a part
That none can bear below:
Chorus

4 It bids my trembling heart rejoice,
It dries each rising tear;
It tells me in a 'still, small voice'
To trust and never fear:
Chorus

5 Jesus, the Name I love so well,
The Name I love to hear!
No saint on earth its worth can tell,
No heart conceive how dear!
Chorus

44

Christ for me, yes, it's Christ for me,
He's my Saviour, my Lord and King;
I'm so happy I shout and sing;
Ev'ry day as I go my way it is Christ for me.

45

1 The Saviour has come in His mighty pow'r,
And spoken peace to my soul,
And all of my life from that very hour
I've yielded to His control,
I've yielded to His control.

Chorus
Wonderful, wonderful, Marvellous and wonderful,
What He has done for my soul!
The half has never been told;
Oh, It is wonderful, It is marvellous and wonderful,
What Jesus has done for this soul of mine!
The half has never been told!

2 From glory to glory He leads me on,
From grace to grace ev'ry day,
And brighter and brighter the glory dawns
While pressing my homeward way,
While pressing my homeward way.
Chorus

3 If fellowship here with my Lord can be
So inexpressibly sweet,
O what will it be when His face we see,
When round the white throne we meet?
When round the white throne we meet?
Chorus

46

1 There's a psalm of praise filling all my days,
Since to Jesus my heart did bow;
O what melody! Glorious harmony!
Life is wonderful now:

Chorus
Life is wonderful, Yes, it's wonderful!
Life is wonderful now to me!
I let Jesus in, He changed ev'rything,
Life is wonderful now!
Since His blessings came into my heart,
Joy unspeakable fills ev'ry part,
And I want to live for my Lord;
Life is wonderful now!

2 All is happiness, gone is my distress,
Peace and vict'ry He does endow;
Since my Saviour came, I can't be the same;
Life is wonderful now:
Chorus

3 All my life is praise for His wondrous grace,
I will serve the Lord, this my vow;
Jesus came to me, and He set me free;
Life is wonderful now:
Chorus

47

Jesus came from heaven with a humble birth,
Took man's form upon Him to live with us on earth.
Jesus grew to manhood in God's perfect plan,
Told us of His Father and His great love for man.
Jesus died at Calv'ry to wash my sins away,
Now He reigns in glory on high,
Jesus lives within me all along life's way,
Jesus came from heaven for me!

48

In my need Jesus found me,
Put His strong arm around me,
Brought me safe home,
Into the shelter of the fold.
Gracious shepherd that sought me,
Precious life-blood that brought me
Out of the night,
Into the light, and nigh to God.

49

Gone! Gone! Gone! Gone! Yes, my sins are gone.
Now my soul is free and in my heart's a song.
Buried in the deepest sea.
Yes, that's good enough for me.
I shall live eternally.
Praise God! my sins are gone.

50

I'm not ashamed, not ashamed of the gospel of Christ
For it is the pow'r of God unto salvation
To ev'ryone, to ev'ryone that believeth.

51

Joined to the vine as a branch of the tree,
Cleansed by His word that He's spoken to me,
Stemmed in His love as He wants me to be:
Bearing the fruit of the Lord.

52

He lives! He lives! Christ Jesus lives today!
He walks with me and talks with me along life's narrow way.
He lives! He lives, salvation to impart!
You ask me how I know He lives – He lives within my heart.

53

Thou shalt guide me with Thy counsel
And after that receive me with glory.
Whom have I in heav'n but Thee,
And who on earth more dear to me?
Thou shalt guide me with Thy counsel
And after that receive me with glory.

54

1 Jesus my Lord will love me for ever,
From Him no pow'r of evil can sever.
He gave His life to ransom my soul,
Now I belong to Him:

Chorus
Now I bring to Jesus,
Jesus belongs to me,
Not for the years of time alone
But for eternity.

2 Once I was lost in sin's degradation,
Jesus came down to bring me salvation,
Lifted me up from sorrow and shame,
Now I belong to Him:
Chorus

3 Joy floods my soul for Jesus has saved me,
Freed me from sin that long had enslaved me,
His precious blood He gave to redeem,
Now I belong to Him:
Chorus

55

1 Who can cheer the heart like Jesus,
By His presence all divine?
True and tender, pure and precious,
O how blest to call Him mine!

Chorus
All that thrills my soul is Jesus;
He is more than life to me, (*to me*),
And the fairest of ten thousand
In my blessed Lord I see.

2 Love of Christ so freely given,
Grace of God beyond degree,
Mercy higher than the heaven,
Deeper than the deepest sea:
Chorus

3 What a wonderful redemption!
Never can a mortal know
How my sin, tho' red like crimson,
Can be whiter than the snow:
Chorus

4 Ev'ry need His hand supplying,
Ev'ry good in Him I see;
On His strength divine relying,
He is all in all to me:
Chorus

5 By the crystal flowing river
With the ransom'd I will sing,
And for ever and for ever
Praise and glorify the King:
Chorus

56

Things are diff'rent now, something happened to me
When I gave my heart to Jesus.

Things are diff'rent now; I was chang'd, it must be,
When I gave my heart to Him.

Things I loved before have passed away,
Things I love far more have come to stay.

57

(*Fellows*): It's an open secret, that Jesus is mine,
(*Girls*): Open secret, Jesus is mine;
(*Fellows*): It's an open secret, this gladness divine;
(*Girls*): Open secret, gladness divine;
(*Fellows*): It's an open secret, I want you to know;
(*Girls*): Secret, secret, Want you to know;
(*Fellows*): It's an open secret, I love my Saviour so.
(*Girls*): Secret, O I love Him so.

And you can seek Him, find Him, Share this secret, too;
Know His loving kindness in ev'rything you do.

(*Fellows*): It's an open secret, I want you to know;
(*Girls*): Secret, secret, want you to know;
(*Fellows*): It's an open secret,
(*Girls*): secret,
I love my Saviour so! so!
Love my Saviour so!

58

1 I would love to tell you what I think of Jesus,
Since I found in Him a Friend so strong and true;
I would tell you how He chang'd my life completely.
He did something that no other friend could do.

Chorus
No one ever cared for me like Jesus.
There's no other friend so kind as He;
No one else could take the sin and darkness from me!
O how much He cared for me.

2 All my life was full of sin when Jesus found me,
All my heart was full of misery and woe;
Jesus placed His strong and loving arms about me,
And He led me in the way I ought to go:
Chorus

3 Ev'ry day he comes to me with new assurance,
More and more I understand His words of love;
But I'll never know just why He came to save me
Till some day I see His blessed face above:
Chorus

59

He gives me satisfying peace, this wonderful Saviour.
He gives me joys that never cease, this wonderful Lord.
'Tis only Jesus who can bless with everlasting happiness,
And He's my Saviour, this wonderful Lord.

60

Jesus is a wonderful Saviour, He will carry you thro',
Jesus is a wonderful Saviour, He will carry you thro', my brother;
Jesus is a wonderful Saviour, He will carry you thro',

And when the battle is done and the victory's won,
My Lord will carry you thro',
And on that last day when you're facing your Maker
You'll need my Jesus to be your Saviour;
He'll ever hide you in the rock of ages,
The rock of ages that was cleft for you,
That was cleft for you.

Love in Jesus, Belinda x
Deut. 31 6 "... He will not fail you or forsake you."

61

1 Jesus is the Saviour whom I love to know,
Heaven is the haven that I'm going to,
Jesus is the captain who now leads my life;
Unworthy as I am I know He came to save
A sinner such as me, a sinner such as me
He came to save from the grave.

Chorus
For God so loved the world that He gave
His only begotten Son
That whosoever believeth on Him should not perish
But have everlasting life.

2 Sometimes when you're feeling all alone and blue,
Jesus can come in and help to pull you through;
Sometimes you just know that you need Jesus too,
So come on, sinner, come to Him, He died for you.
A sinner such as you, a sinner such as me
He came to save from the grave:
Chorus

3 Jesus is the Saviour whom I love to know,
Heaven is the haven where I'm going to go;
Jesus is the captain who now leads my life,
Unworth as I am I know He came to save
A sinner such as me, a sinner such as me
He came to save from the grave.

62

1 Days are filled with gladness, nights are filled with song,
Walking in the King's highway
And the world grows brighter, as we pass along,
Walking in the King's highway.

Chorus
Walking (yes I'm) walking in the King's highway,
Walking in the King's highway (The King's highway),
To the place of many mansions I shall come at last,
Walking in the King's highway.

2 Music from the homeland fills me with delight,
Walking in the King's highway;
Visions of the glory break upon my sight,
Walking in the King's highway.
Chorus

3 Crowned with tender mercies, guarded by His love,
Walking in the King's highway;
Jesus gives a foretaste of the joys above,
Walking in the King's highway.
Chorus

63

1 The King of love my Shepherd is
Whose goodness faileth never,
I nothing lack if I am His
And He is mine for ever.

2 Where streams of living water flow
My ransomed soul He leadeth,
And where the verdant pastures grow
With food celestial feedeth.

3 Perverse and foolish oft I strayed,
But yet in love He sought me,
And on His shoulder gently laid,
And home, rejoicing, brought me.

4 In death's dark vale I fear no ill
With Thee, dear Lord, beside me;
Thy rod and staff my comfort still,
Thy cross before to guide me.

5 Thou spread'st a table in my sight;
Thy unction grace bestoweth;
And O, what transport of delight
From Thy pure chalice floweth!

6 And so through all the length of days
Thy goodness faileth never;
Good Shepherd, may I sing Thy praise
Within Thy house for ever.

64

Rise up and walk! All pow'r is given unto Him,
He changes not, and sin shall not have vict'ry over you.
Rise up and walk! He is the Lord that healeth thee,
At His command thou shalt be free, Christ Jesus
makes you whole!

65

1 There is full salvation through that precious Name:
Jesus came – took our blame;
There is full salvation through that precious Name:
No other name like Jesus.

2 He gives fellowship and guidance all the way:
As we pray – ev'ry day;
He gives fellowship and guidance all the way:
There is no friend like Jesus.

3 Death is swallowed up for all eternity:
Death will be – victory!
Death is swallowed up for all eternity:
We trust a risen Jesus.

4 There is full salvation through that precious Name:
Jesus came – took our blame;
There is full salvation through that precious Name:
No other name like Jesus.

66

Ho! ev'ryone that thirsts in life,
Hear the offer of the Lord;
He is the one who satisfies –
Come of your own accord.
Let the wicked forsake his way
And the unrighteous his thoughts;
Let him return to the Lord our God
And he will find pardon and mercy abundantly!
Seek ye the Lord while He may be found,
Call on Him while He's near;
Find Him as Saviour, Lord and King,
Know Him by love instead of fear.

67

Behold I stand, I stand at the door and knock,
Behold I stand at the door and knock;
If any man will hear My voice let him open the door
And I will come in and sup with him
And he with Me.

68

'Behold I stand, I stand at the door and knock,
Behold I stand, I stand at the door and knock,
If any man will listen to My voice, and open that door,
I will come in.'
This is the invitation that Jesus gives to you,
This is the promise of His Word and it is true.

When He comes in it's fellowship divine,
For I am His and He is mine;
When He comes in, then He will sup with me
Until that day His face I'll see.
This is the invitation that Jesus gives to you,
This is the promise of His Word and it is true.
Behold He stands, He stands at the door and knocks,
Behold He stands, He stands at the door and knocks;
If any man will listen to His voice, and open that door –
He will come in.

69

There's a way back to God from the dark paths of sin;
There's a door that is open and you may go in:
At Calvary's cross is where you begin,
When you come as a sinner to Jesus.

70

1 I heard the voice of Jesus say:
'Come unto Me and rest,
Lay down, thou weary one, lay down
Thy head upon My breast.'
I came to Jesus as I was,
Weary and worn and sad;
I found in Him a resting place
And He has made me glad.

2 I heard the voice of Jesus say:
'Behold, I freely give
The living water: thirsty one,
Stoop down and drink, and live.'
I came to Jesus and I drank
Of that life-giving stream;
My thirst was quenched, my soul revived
And now I live in Him.

3 I heard the voice of Jesus say,
'I am this dark world's light;
Look unto Me, thy morn shall rise,
And all thy days be bright.'
I looked to Jesus and I found
In Him my star, my sun;
And in that light of life I'll walk,
Till travelling days are done.

71

1 Broad is the way that leads man to
The place that's called destruction;
Narrow the way to life anew,
The way which few will walk on:

Chorus
Get on the road which leads you to God,
Start at the cross of Jesus;
He is the way, the truth, and the life –
So trust Him, come and follow Jesus (*Jesus*).

2 God has prepared a place for all
Who trust in Christ as Saviour;
His promise is that at His call
We'll live with Him for ever:
Chorus

3 We can draw near to God in prayer,
Know Him as Friend and Father;
We can approach God without fear,
And know His love for ever:
Chorus

4 No other way to God is true,
No other way than Jesus,
No other way to God for you –
Jesus alone can save us:
Chorus

72

If you want joy, real joy, wonderful joy,
Let Jesus come into your heart.
If you want joy, real joy, wonderful joy,
Let Jesus come into your heart.
Your sins He'll take away,
Your night He'll turn to day,
Your heart He'll make over anew,
And then come in to stay.
If you want joy, real joy, wonderful joy,
Let Jesus come into your heart.

73

Jesus is knocking, patiently waiting,
Outside your heart's closed door.
Do not reject Him, simply accept Him,
Now and for evermore.

74

In Christ there is full salvation,
In Christ there is pow'r o'er sin,
And all who believe on Jesus
Receive His life within.
In Christ there is satisfaction,
In Christ there is joy and rest,
And each hungry soul in Christ made whole
Is ever blest.

75

'Take up the cross thyself deny,
Come boldly after Me.'
The Saviour calls: let us reply,
'Lord, I will follow Thee.'

'Take up the cross, deny yourself,
Come boldly after Me.'
The Saviour calls: Lord, give us grace
To rise and follow Thee.

76

1 Which way are you choosing, the narrow or broad?
You'll have to make up your mind.
Just give up your own way and follow the Lord;
Why don't you make up your mind?
He died, the stranger of Galilee,
To bring salvation to you and me;
A strong companion you'll prove Him to be,
So won't you make up your mind?

2 Which crowd will you follow, the large or the small?
Be sure to make up your mind.
The cost is demanding, but hear Jesus call;
Then come and make up your mind.
Your friends may shun you unthinkingly,
But Christ gives power and liberty;
To life with purpose you'll find the key,
When once you make up your mind!

3 On which are you resting, the Rock or the sand?
You'd better make up your mind!
With Christ as foundation your building will stand,
But have you made up your mind?
Temptations and trials must come your way,
The storms of Judgment will rage one day;
Take Jesus and on Him your confidence stay;
Don't wait, but make up your mind!

4 O what will you do with the Saviour today?
He bids you make up your mind.
Repent and accept Him without delay,
O sinner, make up your mind!
Why stumble alone along the road?
He'll sort your tangles, He'll take your load,
And in your heart He will make His abode;
It's time to make up your mind!

77

1 O there's only one way to heaven, brother,
And you'd better get on that road;
For it leads from Calvary's rugged cross
To the gates of the city of God.
For other roads will lead astray
So take the straight and narrow way;
And you'd better get on that road,
You'd better get on that road.

2 O there's only one way to heaven, brother,
And you'd better get on that road;
For salvation's free, not by works you see,
It is the gift of God's love bestowed.
Your sin on Christ was full laid,
Its penalty is really paid:
So you'd better get on that road,
You'd better get on that road.

3 O there's only one way to heaven, brother,
And you'd better get on that road;
For Christ is the door, and His word is the key
To a home in that blest abode.
He is the Truth, the Life, the Way,
O trust Him now without delay;
And you'd better get on that road;
You'd better get on that road.

78

How long, how long before you come to the Saviour?
Oh sinner, tell me how long.
You know, yes, you know you're lost,
And so to the Saviour you certainly must go.

Well, Jesus died on Calvary to save the lost like you and me;
But still you go on living that way:
Come on now, come under His sway.
So come along, you'll sing that new song, today,
To Jesus come along.

Who can separate us from the love of Christ? Rom. 8.35. God bless you & keep you Love Liz 31.7.74.

79

1 Christian, are you running,
Free from weight of sin,
With the hope before you
A crown of life to win?
Or is your burden heavy,
Each step like backward pace?
How are you progressing
In the Christian race?

2 Where, as you are running,
Do you fix your eyes?
Are they set on Jesus
With faith that never dies?
Or is your vision dazzled
With idols on the way?
How are you progressing
In the race today?

3 Are you ever mindful
Of watchers yet unseen,
Saints of God before you
Who in the race have been?
Or are your thoughts still dwelling
On things the world holds dear?
How are you progressing?–
Keep the vision clear.

4 Christian, press thou onwards,
Looking to the Lord,
Think how His life-blood
Was for thy soul outpoured;
Then leave all burdens with Him,
O never drag that load,
End the race rejoicing,
In that blest abode.

80

1 As you travel along on the Jericho road,
Does the world seem all wrong, and heavy your
load?
Just bring it to Christ, your sins all confess;
On the Jericho road, your heart He will bless.

Chorus
On the Jericho road there's room for just two,
No more and no less, just Jesus and you;
Each burden He'll bear, each sorrow He'll share,
There's never a care, for Jesus is there.

2 On the Jericho road blind Bartimaeus sat,
His life was a void, so empty and flat;
But Jesus appeared, one word brought him sight,
On the Jericho road, Christ banished his night.
Chorus

3 O brother, to you this message I bring,
Though hope may be gone, He'll cause you to sing;
At Jesus' command sin's shackles must fall,
On the Jericho road, will you answer His call?
Chorus

81

1 If any man will follow, if any man will follow,
If any man will follow after my Jesus:
Let him deny himself, oh, let him take up his cross,
And let him come and follow after my Lord!

Whosoever will live for self will throw his life away,
Christ gives life to all who follow Him –
What is a man advantaged if he gains the whole wide world.
And then loses his soul!

2 If any man will follow, if any man will follow,
If any man will follow after my Jesus:
Let him deny himself, oh, let him take up his cross,
And let him some and follow after my Lord!

Whosoever will be ashamed of Jesus and His words,
In this sinful age in which we live,
Jesus the King will be ashamed of him in that great day,
When in glory He comes!

3 If any man will follow, if any man will follow,
If any man will follow after my Jesus,
Let him deny himself, oh, let him take up his cross,
And let him come and follow after my Lord!
Let him come and follow after my Lord.

82

1 I'm glad I'm a Christian,
I'm trusting the Lord;
I rest on God's promise,
Believing His Word.

2 The past is forgiven,
And now I am free;
A mansion in heaven
Is awaiting for me.

3 O come to Jesus,
Your sins all confess;
He's longing to clothe you
In His righteousness.

4 Admit you're a sinner,
Believe He is true;
And when you have found Him
Your life He'll renew.

83

1 Though the world has forsaken God,
Treads a diff'rent path, lives a diff'rent way,
I walk the road that the Saviour trod,
And all may know I live under Jesus' sway:

Chorus
They are watching you, marking all you do,
Hearing the things you say;
Let them see the Saviour as He shines in you,
Let His pow'r control you ev'ry day.

2 Men will look at the life I lead,
See the side I take, and the things I love;
They judge my Lord by my every deed –
Lord, set my affections on things above:
Chorus

3 When assailed in temptation's hour,
By besetting sins, by the fear of man,
Then I can know Jesus' mighty power,
And become like Him in His perfect plan:
Chorus

4 Here on earth people walk in night;
With no lamp to guide, they are dead in sin;
I know the Lord Who can give them light,
I live, yet not I, but Christ within:
Chorus

84

1 If you will follow Jesus
Deny yourself, take up the cross,
And come and follow the Saviour;
Deny yourself, take up the cross,
If you will follow the Lord.

2 If you will follow Jesus
All earthly gain becomes but loss,
If you will follow the Saviour;
All earthly gain becomes but loss
If you will follow the Lord.

3 If you will follow Jesus
You'll really find abundant life,
If you will follow the Saviour;
You'll really find abundant life,
If you will follow the Lord.

4 If you will follow Jesus
Step out in faith upon the way,
And come and follow the Saviour;
Step out in faith upon the way,
And come and follow the Lord.

85

1 There's a time when you travel way back in time;
When you try to unravel, and upwards climb:
Up above the sorrows and scares,
In search of some one who cares,
And you find that God cares for you. . . .

Chorus
He'll see you through;
If you think and pray, simply trust and say,
Come and make my life be new.

2 The place your search leads you to has no escape;
Up a hill to a cross it's true – a grim landscape:
Calvary's the place you're in,
Christ is dying for your sin,
And you know that God cares for you. . . .
Chorus

3 Come with me up to His side and see His face;
Kneel awhile, forget your pride and see His grace:
Hear Him say 'Forgive them all',
Now listen to His call,
And you'll find that God cares for you. . . .
Chorus

4 It is hard for you to understand, but try you must;
As a child takes his father's hand, you must have trust:
Trust in Christ – He died for you –
Believe in this – you know it's true,
That God cares for you. . . .
Chorus

86

1 Not one precious promise of His Word
Ever failed the servants of the Lord,
Tried and proved by many like fine gold,
Sweeter than the honey comb:

Chorus
Never doubt the Word.
God's own precious Word,
Never doubt the Word of God.
There's a promise true
In the Book for you,
Never doubt the Word of God.

2 Ev'ryone who takes God at His Word
Need by doubters never be deterred,
He will find the promise, read or heard,
Never failing to be true:
Chorus

3 Ev'ry promise can be yours or mine
As to Him our minds in prayer incline,
If our hearts have known His love divine
He will want to love Him more:
Chorus

87

1 All Scriptures are given by the breath of God,
Are inspired of God,
Are the Words of the Lord;
All Scriptures are given by the breath of God,
And glorify His Name!

They can make you wise to a saving faith
In Jesus Christ the Lord;
They can make the man of God complete,
And are meant to be his sword!

2 So study to show yourself approved to God,
Fit to use His Word,
Fit to speak in His Name;
So study to show yourself approved to God,
A workman not ashamed.

They'll reprove, correct, and a training in
All righteous living afford;
They will yield up all that we need to know
Of teaching of the Lord!

3 All Scriptures are given by the breath of God,
  Are inspired of God,
  Are the Words of the Lord;
All Scriptures are given by the breath of God,
And glorify His Name!

88

Before you start the day,
Take time alone to pray,
And feed upon God's Word
To know His way;
So start the day with Him,
Then walk the way with Him,
And come to evening time with praise to Him.

89

1 Lord, who left the highest heaven
For a homeless human birth,
And, a child within a stable,
Came to share the life of earth,
With Thy grace and mercy bless
All who suffer homelessness.

2 Lord, who sought by cloak of darkness
Refuge under foreign skies
From the swords of Herod's soldiers,
Ravaged homes, and parents' cries –
May Thy grace and mercy rest
On the homeless and oppressed.

3 Lord, who lived secure and settled,
Safe within the Father's plan,
And in wisdom, stature, favour,
Growing up from boy to man –
May Thy grace and mercy bless
Us with growth in holiness.

4 Lord, who leaving home and kindred,
Followed still as duty led,
Sky the roof and earth the pillow
For the Prince of Glory's head –
With Thy grace and mercy bless
Sacrifice for righteousness.

5 Lord, who in Thy Cross and Passion
Helpless hung 'twixt earth and sky,
Yet whose thoughts were for Thy mother,
And a thief condemned to die –
May Thy grace and mercy rest
On the helpless and distressed.

6 Lord, who rose to life triumphant
With man's whole salvation won,
Risen, glorified, ascended,
All Thy Father's purpose done –
May Thy grace, all conflict past,
Bring Thy children home at last.

90

All your anxiety, all your care,
Bring to the mercy seat, leave it there.
Never a burden He cannot bear,
Never a friend like Jesus.

91

O Lord, teach me to pray,
As I believe on You.
O Lord, teach me to pray,
As I believe on You.
The words to tell you all I would
Are far too few.
Lord, teach me to pray;
But I know You let us bring
Our ev'ry need to You.
Lord, teach us to pray!

92

God hears and He answers pray'r;
Cast on Jesus your ev'ry care,
Trust in His promises, they cannot fail,
For with the Father He'll ever prevail.
God hears and He answers pray'r,
Frees my spirit from all despair;
Hasten to take Him your problems.
For God answers prayer.

93

1 Trust in the Lord, and do not be discouraged,
Trust in the Lord, and stop that feeling blue,
Trust in the Lord, and you will be encouraged,
For Jesus cares for you.

2 Trust in the Lord, and not in any fable,
Trust in the Lord, and find Him wholly true,
Trust in the Lord, and know that He is able
To fill your whole life through.

3 Trust in the Lord, and not in men or nation,
Trust in the Lord, as Saviour, Lord, and King,
Trust in the Lord, for full and free salvation,
And lift your heart and sing.

4 Trust in the Lord, faith is a great adventure,
Trust in the Lord, and never cease to pray,
Trust in the Lord, for all the unknown future,
Today and every day!

94

1 God's will for you is good,
In the pattern of life
Whatsoever each day may bring:
Sing Him your song.

2 God's will for you is good,
Ev'ry morning anew
Think upon His great faithfulness:
Sing Him your song.

3 God's will for you is good,
Stop to ponder again
All the blessings and gifts He gives:
Sing Him your song.

4 God's will for you is good,
Even sorrow and pain
Can bring blessing through His grace:
Sing Him your song.

5 God's will for you is good,
For He sent His own Son
To bear all our guilt and sin:
Sing Him your song.

6 God's will for you is good,
Be it sorrow or joy
He is faithful in life and death:
Sing Him your song.

95

1 I can do all things
Through Christ the Lord who strengthens me;
I can do all things
Through Jesus Christ my King.
For He is the strength of my heart and my soul,
O Jesus, my Saviour;
And He is my friend and my Lord and my all,
O Jesus, my Lord.

2 I can do all things
Through Christ my Lord who strengthens me;
I can do all things
Through Jesus Christ my King.
I'm kept by the pow'r of His sheltering hand,
O Jesus, my Saviour;
He'll bring me at last to that heavenly land,
O Jesus, my Lord.

3 I can do all things
Through Christ my Lord who strengthens me;
I can do all things
Through Jesus Christ, my King!

96

When the road is rough and steep
Fix your eyes upon Jesus,
He alone has pow'r to keep,
Fix your eyes upon Him;
Jesus is a gracious friend,
One on whom you can depend,
He is faithful to the end,
Fix your eyes upon Him.

97

1 Christ be my leader
By night as by day;
Safe through the darkness,
For He is the Way.
Fears for the future
I trust to His care;
Darkness is daylight
When Jesus is there.

2 Christ be my teacher
In age as in youth,
Drifting or doubting,
For He is the Truth.
Grant me to trust Him;
Though shifting as sand,
Doubt cannot daunt me;
In Jesus I stand.

3 Christ be my saviour
In calm as in strife;
Death cannot hold me,
For He is the life.
Nor darkness nor doubting,
Nor sin and its stain,
Can touch my Salvation:
With Jesus I reign.

98

Fellows:

1 When Jesus comes to you
He'll bring gladness, (*Girls:* gladness)
When Jesus comes to you
He'll bring peace; (*Girls:* He'll bring peace)
The glory of His presence,
From care will bring release
When Jesus, Jesus comes to you.

Chorus (All)

When Jesus comes to you,
When Jesus comes to you
He'll fill your heart with gladness.
You'll make others happy too;

Fellows:

2 When Jesus comes to you
He'll bring comfort, (*Girls:* comfort)
When Jesus comes to you
Je'll bring light; (*Girls:* He'll bring light)
The glow of inward courage
Will tinge the darkest night,
When Jesus, Jesus comes to you.

Chorus (All)

When Jesus comes to you,
When Jesus comes to you
He'll fill your heart with gladness,
When Jesus, Jesus comes to you.

99

Christ is the answer to my ev'ry need;
Christ is the answer, He is my friend indeed.
Problems of life my spirit may assail,
With Christ my Saviour I need never fail,
For Christ is the answer to my need.

100

1 When I have sorrow in my heart, what can take it
away?
Only Jesus in my heart can take that sorrow away.

2 When I have fear in my heart, what can take it
away?
Only Jesus in my heart can take that fear away.

3 When I have sin in my heart, what can take it away?
Only Jesus in my heart can take that sin away.

4 When I have Jesus in my heart, what can take Him
away?
(more slowly and with emphasis)
Once take Jesus into my heart, and He has come to
stay.

101

1 I am weak but Thou art strong;
Jesu, keep me from all wrong;
I'll be satisfied as long
As I walk, let me walk, close with Thee;

Chorus
Just a closer walk with Thee,
Grant it, Jesus, this my plea,
Daily walking close with Thee,
Let it be, dear Lord, let it be.

2 Through this world of toils and snares,
If I falter, Lord, who cares?
Who with me my burden shares?
None but Thee, dear Lord, none but Thee:
Chorus

3 When my feeble life is o'er,
Time for me will be no more,
Guide me gently, safely home,
To Thy Kingdom's shore, to Thy shore:
Chorus

102

1 I do not know what lies ahead,
The way I cannot see;
Yet one stands near to be my guide,
He'll show the way to me:

Chorus
I know who holds the future,
And He'll guide me with His hand,
With God things don't just happen,
Ev'rything by Him is planned;
So as I face tomorrow
With its problems large and small
I'll trust the God of miracles,
Give to Him my all.

2 I do not know how many days
Of life are mine to spend;
But one who knows and cares for me
Will keep me to the end:
Chorus

3 I do not know the course ahead,
What joys and griefs are there;
But one is near who fully knows,
I'll trust His loving care:
Chorus

103

Start with chorus
By and by when the morning comes
And all the saints of God are gathering home,
We will hear the story how we've overcome,
And we'll understand it better by and by.

1 Trials dark on ev'ry hand, and we cannot understand
All the ways that God will lead us
To that blessed promised land,
But He'll guide us with His eye
And we'll follow till we die,
And we'll understand it better by and by:
Chorus

2 Temptations, hidden snares, often take us unawares
And our hearts are made to bleed
For each thoughtless word and deed;
And we wonder why the test
When we've tried to do our best,
But we'll understand it better by and by:
Chorus

104

1 Days are filled with sorrow and care,
Hearts are lonely and drear;
Burdens are lifted at Calvary,
Jesus is very near.

Chorus
Burdens are lifted at Calvary,
Calvary, Calvary;
Burdens are lifted at Calvary,
Jesus is very near.

2 Cast your care on Jesus today,
Leave your worry and care;
Burdens are lifted at Calvary,
Jesus is very near.
Chorus

3 Troubled soul, the Saviour can see
Ev'ry heartache and tear;
Burdens are lifted at Calvary,
Jesus is very near.
Chorus

105

1 Only to be what He wants me to be,
Ev'ry moment of ev'ry day;
Yielded completely to Jesus alone,
Ev'ry step of this pilgrim way.

2 Just to be clay in the potter's hands,
Ready to do what His word commands
Only to be what He wants me to be,
Ev'ry moment of ev'ry day.

106

Cleanse me from my sin, Lord,
Put Thy pow'r within, Lord,
Take me as I am, Lord,
And make me all Thine own;
Keep me day by day, Lord,
Underneath Thy sway, Lord,
Make my heart Thy palace
And Thy royal throne.

107

Day by day, dear Lord,
Of Thee three things I pray:
To see Thee more clearly
To love Thee more dearly,
To follow Thee more nearly
Day by day.

108

Spirit of the Living God
Fall afresh on me!
Spirit of the Living God,
Fall afresh on me!
Break me, melt me,
Mould me, fill me!
Spirit of the Living God,
Fall afresh on me!

God is love
God is light
God is faithful
day and night
He is eternal
He never changes
thou the see rises
up to swallow
mountain ranges
Kari S. Nordberg
Norway

109

1 They tried my Lord and Master,
With no one to defend;
Within the halls of Pilate
He stood without a friend:

Chorus

I'll be a friend to Jesus,
My life for Him I'll spend;
I'll be a friend to Jesus
Until my years shall end.

2 The world may turn against Him,
I'll love Him to the end;
And while on earth I'm living,
My Lord shall have a friend:

Chorus

3 I'll do what He may bid me,
I'll go where He may send;
I'll try each flying moment
To prove that I'm His friend:

Chorus

4 To all who need a saviour,
My friend I recommend;
Because He brought salvation
Is why I am His friend:

Chorus

110

Start with Chorus

Bring forth the fruit of the Spirit in your life,
Let the life of Christ be seen in you;
Bring forth the fruit of the Spirit in your life,
And let the Lord be glorified in you.

Seek His patience and His kindness,
Seek His gentleness and self-control,
Seek His goodness and His faithfulness,
And seek most His peace, and joy, and love:
Chorus

111

1 As You cleanse me for today
And forgive my yesterday,
As you cleanse me for today,
I begin anew, Lord.

2 As You've set me in this place
And sufficient is Your grace,
As You've set me in this place,
I begin anew, Lord.

3 As You're watching over me
I can face the enemy,
As You're watching over me,
I begin anew, Lord.

4 As I'm ever in Your sight
In the depth or in the height,
As I'm ever in Your sight,
I begin anew, Lord.

112

1 O Holy Spirit, giver of life,
You bring our souls immortality;
Yet in our hearts is struggle and strife,
We need your inward vitality;
Work out within us the Father's design,
Give to us life, O Spirit Divine.

2 O Holy Spirit, giver of light,
To minds where all is obscurity;
Exchange for blindness, spiritual sight,
That we may grow to maturity;
Work out within us the Father's design,
Give to us light, O Spirit Divine.

3 O Holy Spirit, giver of love,
And joy, and peace, and fidelity;
The fruitfulness which comes from above,
That self-control and humility;
Work out within us the Father's design,
Give to us love, O Spirit Divine.

113

1 There is a place of quiet rest,
Near to the heart of God,
A place where sin cannot molest,
Near to the heart of God.

Chorus

O Jesus, blest Redeemer,
Sent from the heart of God,
Hold us, who wait before Thee,
Near to the heart of God.

2 There is a place of comfort sweet,
Near to the heart of God,
A place where we our Saviour meet,
Near to the heart of God.

Chorus

3 There is a place of full release,
Near to the heart of God,
A place where all is joy and peace,
Near to the heart of God:

Chorus

114

According to the working of His mighty pow'r,
We are raised up together with Christ.
According to the pleasure of His holy will,
We are sanctified.
According to the riches of His glory and His grace,
He supplies our ev'ry need,
So that henceforth we might live only unto Him.
Our friend and Lord indeed.

115

Lord, make me useful to Thee,
Send now Thy spirit to me,
They perfect will
In me fulfil,
Lord, make me useful to Thee.

116

1 His hands were pierced, the hands that made
The mountain range and everglade;
That washed the stains of sin away
And changed earth's darkness into day.

2 His feet were pierced, the feet that trod
The furthest shining star of God;
And left their imprint deep and clear
On ev'ry winding pathway here.

3 His heart was pierced, the heart that burned
To comfort ev'ry heart that yearned;
And from it came a cleansing flood,
The river of redeeming blood.

4 His hands and feet and heart, all three
Were pierced for me on Calvary;
And here and now, to Him I bring
My hands, feet, heart, an offering.

117

1 Though days are long, oft filled with care,
Though burdens seem so hard to bear;
No matter what my lot may be,
I'll live for Him who died for me:

Chorus

I'll live for Jesus day after day,
I'll live for Jesus let come what may,
The Holy Spirit I will obey,
And live for Jesus day after day.

2 Through ev'ry day new joy I find.
He gives to me real peace of mind,
Until the day when Christ I'll see,
I'll live for Him who died for me:

Chorus

118

1 Creator God, Creator God!
With Thee I am a man,
But without Thee, O Lord my Saviour,
Without Thee I am just a child.

2 Creator God, Creator God!
With Thy hands may I work,
With Thy feet may I walk, O Saviour,
And through Thine own eyes let me see.

3 And with Thy heart, Creator God,
I will learn and love,
With Thy heart, O Creator God
I'll learn and love like Thee.

119

I'll live for Christ who gave Himself on the tree,
I'm crucified with Christ whose death set me free,
And yet I live, for Christ is living in me:

I'll live for Christ alway,
I'll live for Christ alway,
I'll serve Him ev'ry day;
I'll live by faith in Christ and trust in His grace;
I'll live for Christ alway.

120

Version 1

Give me oil in my lamp, keep me burning,
Give me oil in my lamp, I pray;
Give me oil in my lamp, keep me burning,
Keep me burning 'til the break of day:

Chorus

Sing Hosanna! Sing Hosanna!
Sing Hosanna to the King of Kings!
Sing Hosanna! Sing Hosanna!
Sing Hosanna to the King.

(N.B. *2 part chorus – One group sustain* '*Sing*' *while the other group does* '*Sing Hosanna*', *etc.*)

Version 2

1 Give me joy in my heart, keep me praising,
Give me joy in my heart, I pray;
Give me joy in my heart, keep me praising,
Keep me praising 'til the break of day:
Chorus as version 1

2 Give me peace in my heart, keep me resting . . .
Chorus

3 Give me love in my heart, keep me serving . . .
Chorus

Jesus is wonderful. With love from Sissel Bremnes from Norway Oslo.

Version 3

1 What a wonderful Saviour is Jesus,
What a wonderful friend is He,
For He left all the glory of heaven,
Came to earth to die on Calvary:

Chorus as version 1

2 He arose from the grave, Hallelujah,
And He lives never more to die.
At the Father's right hand interceding,
He will hear and heed our faintest cry:

Chorus

3 He is coming some day to receive us,
We'll be caught up to heaven above,
What a joy it will be to behold Him,
Sing forever of His grace and love:

Chorus

121

1 I want to walk with Jesus Christ,
All the days I live of this life on earth,
To give to Him complete control
Of body and of soul:

Chorus

Follow Him, follow Him, yield your life to Him,
He has conquered death, He is King of Kings,
Accept the joy which He gives to those
Who yield their lives to Him.

2 I want to learn to speak to Him,
To pray to Him, confess my sin,
To open my life and let Him in,
For joy will then be mine:

Chorus

3 I want to learn to speak of Him,
My life must show that He lives in me,
My deed, my thoughts, my words must speak
All of His love for me:

Chorus

4 I want to learn to read His Word,
For this is how I know the way
To live my life as pleases Him,
In holiness and joy:

Chorus

5 O Holy Spirit of the Lord,
Enter now into this heart of mine,
Take full control of my selfish will
And make me wholly Thine:

Chorus

122

1 O when you come to the end of life's journey,
Weary and worn, and the battle is done,
Carrying the Cross, the Cross of redemption,
He'll understand and say 'Well done',
He'll understand and say 'Well done'.

2 Give, when you give, the best of your service,
Telling the world that the Saviour has come;
Be not dismayed if men won't defend you,
He'll understand and say 'Well done',
He'll understand and say 'Well done'.

3 O when you try, and fail in your trying,
Hands sore and scarred from the work you have begun,
Come to the cross, come quickly to Jesus,
He'll understand and say 'Well done',
He'll understand and say 'Well done'.

123

1 Looking unto Jesus
Who has gone before,
Now enthroned in glory,
King for evermore.
Born again of His Spirit,
Saved by His shed blood,
Given work to be done for Him,
Joined to Him by love:

Chorus
Looking unto Jesus
Who has gone before,
Now enthroned in glory,
King for evermore.

2 Looking unto Jesus,
In the Christian fight,
Seeking grace to witness,
Strengthened by His might,
With the armour of Jesus,
With the Spirit's sword,
With much prayer that He'll bless His Word,
Fighting for the Lord:
Chorus

3 Looking unto Jesus
Who despised the shame,
Throwing off all hindrance
As we bear His Name.
Help us face all temptation,
Lord, help us discern,
Give us courage to speak for Thee,
Help our light to burn:
Chorus

124

O Jesus, Lord and Saviour, I give myself to Thee;
For Thou, in Thy atonement, didst give Thyself for me;
I own no other master, my heart shall be Thy throne;
My life I give, henceforth to live, O Christ, for Thee alone.

125

1 I have decided to follow Jesus,
I have decided to follow Jesus,
I have decided to follow Jesus,
No turning back, no turning back.

2 The cross before me, the world behind me,
The cross before me, the world behind me,
The cross before me, the world behind me,
No turning back, no turning back.

126

1 Lord Jesus Christ,
You have come to us,
You are one with us,
Mary's Son.
Cleansing our souls from all their sin,
Pouring Your love and goodness in,
Jesus, our love for You we sing,
Living Lord.

At Communion
2 Lord Jesus Christ,
Now and every day,
Teach us how to pray,
Son of God,
You have commanded us to do
This in remembrance, Lord, of You:
Into our lives Your power breaks through,
Living Lord.

3 Lord Jesus Christ,
You have come to us,
Born as one of us,
Mary's Son.
Led out to die on Calvary,
Risen from death to set us free,
Living Lord Jesus, help us see
You are Lord.

4 Lord Jesus Christ,
I would come to You,
Live my life for You,
Son of God.
All Your commands I know are true,
Your many gifts will make me new,
Into my life Your power breaks through,
Living Lord.

P. Appleford

127

1 To Him we come:
Jesus Christ our Lord,
God's own living Word,
His dear Son.
In Him there is no east and west,
In Him all nations shall be blest,
To all He offers peace and rest,
Loving Lord.

2 In Him we live:
Christ our strength and stay,
Life, and Truth, and Way,
Friend divine.
His power can break the chains of sin,
Still all life's storms without, within,
Help us the daily fight to win,
Living Lord.

3 For Him we go:
Soldiers of the cross,
Counting all things loss,
Him to know;
Going to men of every race,
Preaching to all His wondrous grace,
Building His Church in every place,
Conquering Lord.

4 With Him we serve:
His the work we share
With saints everywhere.
Near and far;

One in the task which faith requires,
One in the zeal which never tires,
One in the hope His love inspires,
Coming Lord.

5 Onward we go,
Faithful, bold, and true,
His blest will to do,
Day by day.
Till, at the last, with joy, we'll see
Jesus, in glorious majesty;
Live with Him through eternity,
Reigning Lord!

128

Ev'ry person in ev'ry nation
In each succeeding generation
Has the right to hear the news
That Christ can save.

Crucified on Calv'ry's mountain
He opened wide a cleansing fountain,
Conquered sin and death and hell,
He rose up from the grave.

Father, I am willing to dedicate to Thee
Life and talent, time and money:
Here am I, send me.

129

1 A vessel called the Church of God
Sails over time's great sea;
She sets her course for God's great port
To God's eternity.
The world attacks her like a storm,
There's danger, need, and fear;
She sails with hope and victory
Through ev'ry passing year.

The question constantly is asked,
Can this great ship endure?
Can she survive the world's attacks?
Is victory secure?

Chorus
We can triumph, Lord,
As You stay with us, Lord,
We will sail on the turbulent sea of this life
And sail with You as Lord!

2 What happens if the ship remains
At moorings by the quay?
What happens if she wants the calm
And will not put to sea?
    It may be nice to glory in
    The vict'ries of the past,
    But God wants us to sail today –
    His colours at the mast!
The course of God is sacrifice,
We must not fear the cost;
The life not lived for Christ the Lord
Is life which God calls lost:
Chorus

3 The ship we call the Church of God
Depends upon its crew;
There are no passengers aboard,
There's work for all to do.
    God has a post for ev'ryone,
    A duty to fulfil;
    He gifted us, now looks to us,
    To do His perfect will.
We work together as a team
With fellowship in Him,
We have a common faith and hope –
The Spirit's power within:
Chorus

4 The ship has many would-be guides
Who state what course they think;
They rest upon man's thought alone
And with them we would sink!

But God has made His course quite clear,
His way is in His Word;
We see the fulness of the truth
As we look to the Lord.
When onslaughts come upon our faith
Let courage flood our hearts;
We are a world-wide fellowship
And share all God imparts:
Chorus

130

1 There's a road which leads from Jerusalem,
It's the way down to Jericho,
It's Compassion road, steep and tiring road,
Which has danger from thieving foe.
And here on this road is one man
Beaten up and left as half dead,
Like many in this world around us
Oppressed, in despair or unfed.
Hear him cry out
As he lies on Compassion road.

2 Watch a priest and Levite come down that road
Only giving the man small heed,
They are too caught up with religious thoughts
To give help to a man in need.
Samaritan, walk behind them!
You are not within the same class!
But you are the one who helps him –
You could not see need and just pass!
You heard the cry
As you walked on Compassion road.

3 The Compassion road goes right on through life,
It's a road with us still today,
Many hands are needed to give the help
To those stricken upon the way.
So now will you have compassion?

To the lonely, hungry, and worn,
To those without hope or salvation,
To fearful and poor and forlorn?
Lord, give us grace
To give help on Compassion road.

131

1 The fields are white unto harvest time,
Look up and see!
The fields are white unto harvest time,
Look up and see:

Chorus
Pray to the Lord of the harvest,
Christ says pray.
Pray to the Lord for the workers
Which we need in this day.

2 The harvest truly is fit to reap
But workers few,
The harvest truly is fit to reap
But workers few:
Chorus

3 Who else will 'go into all the world'
To preach the Word?
Who else will 'go into all the world'
To preach the Word?
Chorus

4 The Lord's return may be very soon,
The time is short!
The Lord's return may be very soon,
The time is short:
Chorus

132

1 Go forth and tell! O Church of God, awake!
God's saving news to all the nations take.
Proclaim Christ Jesus, Saviour, Lord, and King,
That all the world His worthy praise may sing.

2 Go forth and tell! God's love embraces all:
He will in grace respond to all who call.
How shall they call if they have never heard
The gracious invitation of His Word?

3 Go forth and tell! Men still in darkness lie:
In wealth or want, in sin they live and die.
Give us, O Lord, concern of heart and mind,
A love like Thine which cares for all mankind.

4 Go forth and tell! The doors are open wide:
Share God's good gifts with men so long denied.
Live out your life as Christ, your Lord, shall choose,
Your ransomed powers for His sole glory use.

5 Go forth and tell! O Church of God, arise:
Go in the strength which Christ your Lord supplies.
Go, till all nations His great Name adore
And serve Him Lord and King for evermore.

133

1 O when the saints go marching in,
O when the saints go marching in;
O Lord, I want to be among the number
When the saints go marching in.

2 O when they crown Him Lord of all,
O when they crown Him Lord of all;
O Lord, I want to be among the number
When they crown Him Lord of all.

3 O when all knees bow at His name,
O when all knees bow at His name;
O Lord, I want to be among the number
When all knees bow at His name.

4 O when they sing the Saviour's praise,
O when they sing the Saviour's praise;
O Lord, I want to be among the number
When they sing the Saviour's praise.

5 O when the saints go marching in,
O when the saints go marching in;
O Lord, I want to be among the number
When the saints go marching in.

134

1 I gotta home in gloryland that outshines the sun,
I gotta home in gloryland that outshines the sun,
I gotta home in gloryland that outshines the sun,
Way beyond the blue:

Chorus
Do Lord, oh, do Lord, oh, do remember me;
Do Lord, oh, do Lord, oh, do remember me;
Do Lord, oh, do Lord, oh, do remember me;
Way beyond the blue.

2 I took Jesus as my Saviour,
you take Him too . . .

3 If you will not bear a cross,
you can't wear a crown . . .

Alternative version
1 I gotta home in gloryland that outshines the sun,
I gotta home in gloryland that outshines the sun,
I gotta home in gloryland that outshines the sun,
Way beyond the blue:

Chorus
Thank You, my Saviour, for that eternal life;
Thank You, my Saviour, for that eternal life;
Thank You, my Saviour, for that eternal life
With You evermore!

2 Those who trust in Christ as Saviour,
shall never die . . .

3 If you will not bear a cross,
you can't wear a crown . . .

135

1 When I come to the river at ending of day
When the last winds of sorrow have blown,
There'll be somebody waiting to show me the way,
I won't have to cross Jordan alone:

Chorus
I won't have to cross Jordan alone,
Jesus died for my sins to atone;

(*solo*) When the darkness I see, He'll be waiting for me,
I won't have to cross Jordan alone.

2 Oftentimes I'm forsaken, and weary and sad
When it seems that my friends have all gone,
There is one thought that cheers me and makes my heart glad,
I won't have to cross Jordan alone:
Chorus

3 Though the billows of sorrow and trouble may sweep,
Christ the Saviour will care for His own;
Till the end of the journey, my soul He will keep,
I won't have to cross Jordan alone:
Chorus

136

1 This world is not my home,
I'm just a-passing through;
My treasures are laid up
Somewhere beyond the blue;
The Saviour beckons me
From heaven's open door,
And I can't feel at home
In this world any more.

Chorus
O Lord, you know, I have no friend like you;
If heaven's not my home, then Lord what will I do?
The Saviour beckons me from heaven's open-door,
And I can't feel at home in this world any more.

2 They're all expecting me,
And that's one thing I know,
My Saviour pardoned me,
Now onward I must go;
I know He'll take me through
Though I am weak and poor,
And I can't feel at home
In this world any more.
Chorus

3 Just over in glory land
We'll live eternally,
The saints on every hand
Are shouting victory;
Their songs of sweetest praise
Drift back from heaven's shore,
And I can't feel at home
In this world any more.
Chorus

137

Start with Chorus
O sinner man, where will you run to?
O sinner man, where will you run to?
O sinner man, where will you run to
All on that day?

1 Run to the rocks, rocks won't you hide me?
Run to the rocks, rocks won't you hide me?
Run to the rocks, rocks won't you hide me,
All on that day?
Chorus

2 Run to the sea, sea is a-boiling,
Run to the sea, sea is a-boiling,
Run to the sea, sea is a-boiling,
All on that day.
Chorus

3 Run to the Lord, Lord won't you hide me?
Run to the Lord Lord won't you hide me?
Run to the Lord, Lord won't you hide me,
All on that day.
Chorus

4 O sinner man, should bin a-praying,
O sinner man, should bin a-praying,
O sinner man, should bin a-praying,
All on that day.
Chorus

138

(*solo*)
1 If religion were a thing
(*Everyone else*) *If religion were a thing*
That money could buy,
That money could buy
Then the rich would live
Then the rich would live
And the poor would die:
And the poor would die

Chorus
All my sins be taken away,
All glory be to His Name,
All sins be taken away,
Be taken away,

2 Christ died for us all, He died upon the tree,
But now He lives, He lives in me:
Chorus

3 We praise Thee, O God, we acknowledge Thee
To be the Lord, the Lord most high:
Chorus

Alternative version

1 Our Father which are in heaven,
Hallowed be Thy Name; Thy kingdom come.
Chorus

2 Thy will be done in earth as in heaven,
Put us not to the test, lead us not into wrong.
Chorus

139

1 You've got to walk that lonesome valley,
You've got to walk there by yourself;
And no one here can walk there for you,
You've got to walk there by yourself.

2 You've got to face one day your Maker,
You've got to face Him by yourself;
And no one here can face Him for you,
You've got to face Him by yourself.

3 You've got to stand one day in Judgment,
You've got to stand there by yourself;
And no one here can stand there for you,
You've got to stand there by yourself.

4 You've got to walk that lonesome valley,
You've got to walk there by yourself;
And no one here can walk there for you,
You've got to walk there by yourself.

140

1 Where you there when they crucified my Lord?
Where you there when they crucified my Lord?
Oh! Sometimes it causes me to tremble, tremble,
tremble.
Were you there when they crucified my Lord?

2 Were you there when they nailed Him to the tree?

3 Were you there when they pierced Him in the side?

4 Were you there when the sun refused to shine?

5 Were you there when they laid Him in the tomb?

6 Were you there when He rose up from the dead?
Were you there when He rose up from the dead?
O-o-oh! Sometimes I feel like shouting glory, glory, glory!
Were you there when He rose up from the dead?

141

1 Steal away, steal away,
Steal away to Jesus;
Steal away, steal away home,
I ain't got long to stay here.

Chorus
My Lord He calls me;
He calls me by the thunder;
The trumpet sounds within my soul.
I ain't got long to stay here.

2 Green trees are bending,
The sinner stands a-trembling;
The trumpet sounds within my soul;
I ain't got long to stay here.
Chorus

3 My Lord He calls me;
He calls me by the lightning;
The trumpet sounds within my soul;
I ain't got long to stay here:
Chorus

142

Start with chorus
Is there anybody here who loves my Jesus?
Anybody here who loves my Lord?
I want to know, yes, I want to know,
Do you love my Lord?

1 I want to sing that I love my Jesus;
I want to shout that I love my Lord:
I want to know, yes, I want to know,
Do you love my Lord?
Chorus

2 Makes us feel like shouting when you love my Jesus;
Makes us fell like shouting when you love my Lord:
I want to know, yes, I want to know,
Do you love my Lord?
Chorus

3 Shout it from the mountains if you love my Jesus:
Sing it in the valleys if you love my Lord:
I want to know, yes, I want to know,
Do you love my Lord?
Chorus

143

N.B. Some sing as the chorus:
Little David followed the Lord,
Why don't you? Why don't you?

Start with chorus
Little David, play on your harp,
Hallelu, Hallelu,
Little David, play on your harp,
Hallelu.

1 Little David was a shepherd boy;
He killed Goliath, shouted for joy:
Chorus

2 Joshua was the son of Nun,
He never would quit till the work was done:
Chorus

144

1 The gospel train's a-coming, I hear it close at hand,
I hear those car wheels rumbling and moving through the land:

Chorus
Get on board, little children, get on board,
Little children, get on board, little children,
There's room for many'a more.

2 I hear the bell and whistle, a-coming round the curve,
She's playing all the steam and power, and straining every nerve:
Chorus

3 The fare is cheap and all can go, the rich and poor and there,
No second class aboard that train, no difference in the fare:
Chorus

4 No signal for another train to follow on the line,
O sinner, you're for ever lost if once you're left behind:
Chorus

She's nearing now the station – O sinner, don't be vain;
O come and get your ticket, and be ready for that train:
Chorus

145

1 Lord, I want to be a Christian in my heart, in my heart,
Lord, I want to be a Christian in my heart,
In my heart, in my heart,
Lord I want to be a Christian in my heart.

2 Lord, I want to be more loving in my heart . . .

3 Lord, I want to be more holy in my heart . . .

4 Lord, I want to be like Jesus in my heart . . .

146

Start with chorus
Joshua fought the battle of Jericho,
Jericho, Jericho,
Joshua fought the battle of Jericho.
And the walls came a-tumbling down.

1 You may talk of your King of Gibeon,
You may talk of your man of Saul,
There's none like good old Joshua,
And the battle of Jericho:
Chorus

2 Up to the walls of Jericho
He marched with spear in hand,
'Go blow them rams horns', Joshua cried,
'For the battle is in my hand.'
Chorus

3 Then the lam rams sheephorns begin to blow,
Trumpets began to sound;
Joshua commanded the people to shout.
And the walls came a-tumbling down:
Chorus

147

1 Goin' to lay down my burden
Down by the riverside,
Down by the riverside,
Down by the riverside;
Goin' to lay down my burden
Down by the riverside.
And grieve my Lord no more:

Chorus
Ain't goin' to grieve my Lord no more,
Ain't goin' to grieve my Lord no more,
Ain't goin' to grieve my Lord no more,
Ain't goin' to grieve my Lord no more,
Ain't goin' to grieve my Lord no more,
Ain't goin' to grieve my Lord no more.

2 Goin' to lay down my sword and shield . . .
3 Goin' to try on my long white robe . . .
4 Goin' to try on my starry crown . . .

Alternative version

1 Goin' to lay down my burden . . .
2 Goin' to sing for my Saviour . . .
3 Goin' to talk to my Maker . . .
4 Goin' to follow my Master . . .

148

1 Somebody's knocking at your door,
Somebody's knocking at your door;
O sinner, why don't you answer?
Somebody's knocking at your door.

2 Knocks like Jesus,
Somebody's knocking at your door;
Knocks like Jesus,
Somebody's knocking at your door.
O sinner, why don't you answer?
Somebody's knocking at your door.

3 Can't you hear Him?
Somebody's knocking at your door;
Can't you hear Him?
Somebody's knocking at your door.
O sinner, why don't you answer?
Somebody's knocking at your door.

4 Answer Jesus,
Somebody's knocking at your door;
Answer Jesus,
Somebody's knocking at your door.
O sinner, why don't you answer?
Somebody's knocking at your door.

149

Start with chorus
There is a balm in Gilead
To make the wounded whoie,
There is a balm in Gilead
To heal the sin-sick soul.

1 Sometimes I feel discouraged
And think my work's in vain,
But then the Holy Spirit
Revives my soul again:
Chorus

2 You cannot sing like angels,
You cannot preach like Paul,
But you can tell of Jesus
And say He died for all:
Chorus

Start with chorus
Go tell it on the mountain
Over the hills and ev'rywhere;
Go tell it on the mountain
That Jesus Christ is Lord.

1 Oh, when I was a seeker
I sought both night and day;
I asked the Lord to help me,
And He showed me the way:
Chorus

2 He made me a watchman,
Upon the city wall;
To tell of His salvation
For Jesus died for all:
Chorus

3 Go tell it to your neighbour
In darkness here below;
Go with the words of Jesus,
That all the world may know:
Chorus

Wenn Du schläfst, schlafe
richtig oder alleine, aber
auf jeden Fall langweile
Dich nicht dabei